Copyright@ March 2018

Living Letter Lessons
All Rights Reserved
Printed in The United States of America

Author Peggy Louise Parrish
Cover Illustrations Peggy Louise Parrish
Interior Illustrations Peggy Louise Parrish

ISBN -13   978-198 6128742

Living Letters Lesson

A Unique Workbook of Creative Lettering

By Peggy Louise Parrish

C. 2018

LIVING LETTERS INTRODUCTION
Words by the author Peggy Parrish

This is a book of art instruction for creative lettering.
I have named the lettering Living Letters because I decided the letters look alive with various plants and living things. It is my hope that you will learn techniques from me that will enhance the lettering you already do. If you keep trying out these ideas you will soon be designing your own style of letters.

*Have fun relaxing in your "sit down" time. Try out some of the techniques of this book.
*Let your doodling habit take on new excitement as these techniques become apart of you.
Living Letters can become a rewarding way to relax, a creative form of expression and awake your art skills to a new level.

Take these instructions, an ink gel pen, some paper and "let it flow."
You will learn both the "graceful loop" methods and the step by step techniques of the "designer touches" (embellishments). Plants, insects, birds, and flowers can become apart of your letters as well. They will appear to be on top of, part of, behind and in front of your letters.

One rule is practice, practice, practice. But please don't treat it like a chore. It should be like a discovery. You will surprise yourself at what you pick up in a short time.

Enjoy the journey of designing "Living Letters".

The LIVING LETTERS LESSON BOOK
By Peggy Parrish

LIVING LETTERS

TABLE OF CONTENTS

Living Letters Introduction

Lesson 1 Graceful Loop Instruction

Lesson 2 Making "The Rose"

Lesson 3 Adding the Side Loops

Lesson 4 Straight "Graceful Loop" Letters

Lesson 5 Curvy "Graceful Loop" Letters

Lesson 6 Embellishments (Designer Touches)

Part 1 Dots
Part 2 Dashes
Part 3 The Curly
Part 4 Windows
Part 5 Eyelet
Part 6 Pasley
Part 7 Ropes and Trims

Lesson 7 Shadowing and Dimensioning

Lesson 8 Designer Lettering

Lesson 9 Creative Coloring

Lesson 10 Lettering Choices

Lesson 11 Living Touches (nature touches)

*The Last Assignment

Lesson 1 The Basic GRACEFUL LOOP Instuction

The Graceful Loop is a type of lettering that is made piece by piece.
Graceful loops are made designing as you go, step by step. I start at the top left of the letters that are straight line letters. This would be the ADEFHIKLMNPRTVWXYandZ letters.
The more rounded letters BCGJOPQSandU I start at the top but not always in the same position. As you get used to making these loops you will start to find ease designing them in your own style. Remember you can make them thin, fat or inbetween in width. You can draw them short, tall or medium in height. Consider your paper, space and the artistic impression you are after.
*I highly recommend a fine tip ink gel pen. Pentel is the one I use. There are others that will work well. I don't find the extra fine tip to be my favorite in the formation of the letters. However both the extra fine ink gel and the Sharpie black marker come in very handy for add-ons. When coloring in your letters colored pencils are the most suitable. There may be times when markers, color crayons and ink gel glitter pens would also help your lettering. A ruler and a pencil are good for drawing the line your letters go on.
Erase the pencil lines after the ink gel is dry and before coloring.

To begin the Graceful Loop style letters draw several teardrop shapes like this one.

Now draw what resembles a teardrop going up:

Go back inside the teardrop and draw an opening like this:

Go back in the upward teardrop and draw a similar opening.

A simple curl to start the teardrop always helps the letter.
Practice a few loops with curls.

PLP

Lesson 2 Add a piece of creation. Our example is THE ROSE.

We will be adding this rose to the bottom of our loop. In further lessons you will find there is no rule that you must pick a rose for this spot. You may pick several roses, another flower or even another creature to draw there. In our drawing of "Living Letters" we are attempting to show living things coming thru and around our lettering. This makes them look very alive. Later on you will find great fun choosing your own add ons. For now let's get real practiced at the rose.

1. Make one row of circles

2. Make one row of circles like this one

3. Make one row of circles with these two marks

4. Make one row of circles with these three marks

5. Now try to make a rose leaf like this:

6. Make your Lesson 1 downward teardrop loop and add a rose with 2 leaves at the bottom.

PLP

7. Make your Lesson 1 upward teardrop and add a rose with 2 leaves at the bottom.

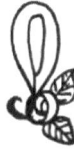 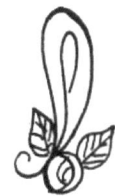

Add another graceful loop(teardrop shape) to the bottom of the rose.

It is best to interface the opposite direction teardrop loop to the other teardrop shape. Putting either the two bottoms of loops facing each other or the two tops together. Here is an example:

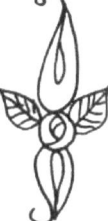

Try several like this one.

Can you try 2 loops with 3 roses inbetween with leaves?

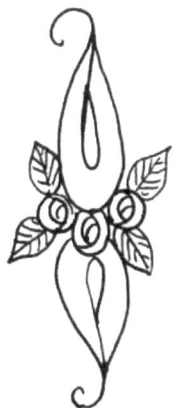

PLP

Lesson 3 The Side Loops

We could at this point at contruct a B,D, E,F,H,I,K,L,M,N,P,R,orT.
We are only going to make the letter "K" at this time. So start the side loops of the letter.
Start with the top right loop construction. Let's try with a slight curl making the downward tear drop from the far right down into the rose area. Land the teardrop shape into the 2 loops joined with the rose part of the letter.
It will look like this:

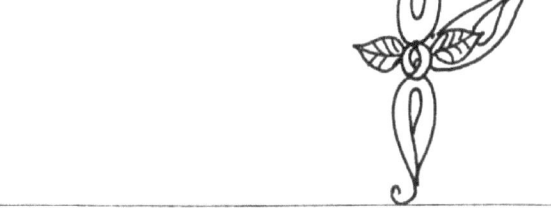

Would you try to make a row of your own?

Now we need to make the bottom right side. Start at the rose area and direct your loop out from there.

It will look something like this.

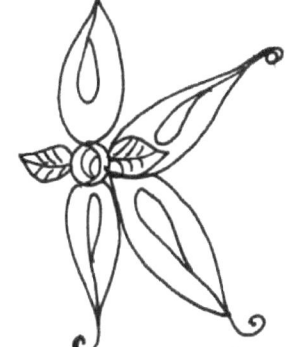

Try some of your own.

PLP

Lesson 4 Other examples of straight "Graceful Loop" Letters.

*Try to make a letter "T" with two open teardrop loops facing each other with roses inbetween.
Start from the left and move right.
Then do the bottom loop below the roses.*

Here is an example.

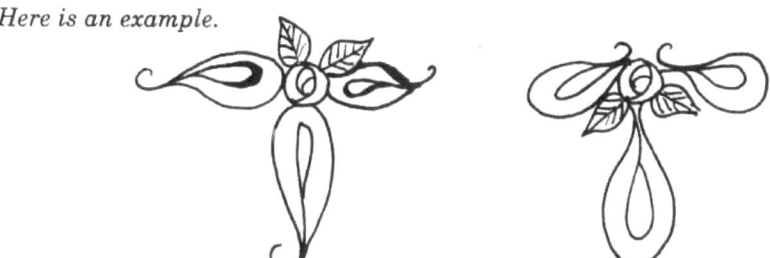

Try some of your own now.

Try the letter "V".

Try first to draw two downward tears meeting at the base of the angle with a rose.

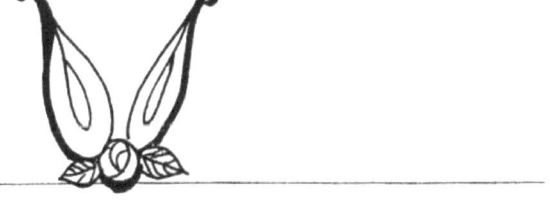

Try some of these:

PLP

Lesson 5 CURVY GRACEFUL LOOPS

At first you may want to pencil out where you think your loops will be before doing them in ink gel. They are a little harder than the straight letters to picture when you first start. There are no rules of whether to start with the small end of the teardrop loop or the big end. As you go along you will find which look you like best. Experiment with all the combinations. For instance in a letter "C" you can use 1, 2 or 3 loops, depending what you like. Some letters have both staight and curvy parts(B,D,J,P,R,) For these letters just combine what you learned in the "straight" lesson with the "curvy" lesson.

Here is an example of a "C" with one loop, 2 loops and 3 loops.

Try one of each.

My very favorite letter is the letter"S"

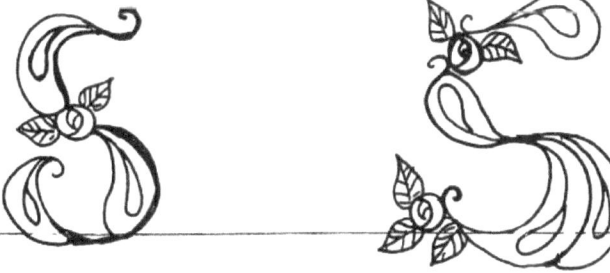

Can you reproduce one of each of these ?

PLP

Lesson 6 EMBELLISHMENTS (Fancy Add-ons)

This is a very fun section. These "Fancies" are only a few of the possibilities you can add to your letters. I'll bet in time you'll find your own little drawing secrets to add on.
Keep doodling whenever you get the chance. Experiment adding on the embellishments I will now describe. Feel free after you practice these to add on your own.

Part 1 DOTS

Dots are very cute to use either by themselves around a letter, inside a letter or out in the space near a letter doing artsy curves and lines. If an outline is put around them dots take on still another "look".

Here is a plain "N" with dots lining it. Don't those dots dress it up?

Can you make one like it?

Now try the same "N" with dots lined with an outer line.

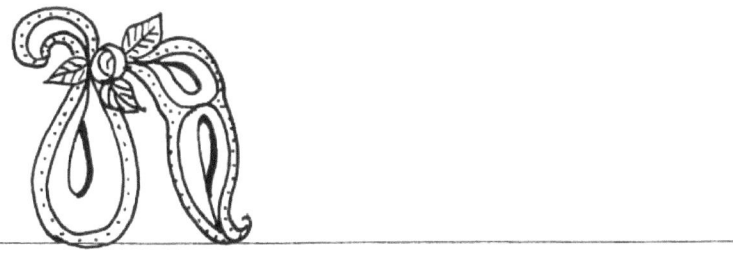

Try to reproduce an "N" like this one.

PLP

*Please feel free to try practicing any and all letters not mentioned with the embellishments which we are describing. Get out your scrap paper and clip board and ENJOY!

Can you make a rose and put dots on it?

Remember dots can be small and cute or big and beautiful on the Graceful Loop Letters. It depends on the impression you are trying to make with your letters.

Part 2 DASHES

Dashes can be used similar to dots. They are especially nice if you want your letters to look like material with stitches.
Practice a few lines of dashes. You might even want to call them "stitches".

Can you copy this?

Both dash techniques will come in handy to add character to your lettering.

Here is an "O" with cute dashes or stitches.

Can you make one like this one as well as one that you make up?

Part 3 CURLY (THE CURLICUE)

A Curly can go forwards or backwards. It can start or finish a letter. It can also be added for extra character.

Notice the Curly lines here:

Practice:

Part 4 WINDOWS

Windows are what I call an opening drawn in your lettering. They are the larger "negative spaces" or blank spaces left in the letters. They are not colored in. They may be round, angular or odd shaped. You may like to experiment with the "look" that different shapes leave.

Here are some examples:

PLP

Can you try these examples and one of your own?

Part 5 EYELET

Eyelet is what I have named the smaller holes or "windows" in the letters.
Eyelet is especially nice in patterns. You may want to get some ideas from the patterns
you find in eyelet material. When you draw in your Eyelet pattern of holes, remember do not color the
holes in. The blank spaces will make the rest of the letter "pop" with color.

Here is an example: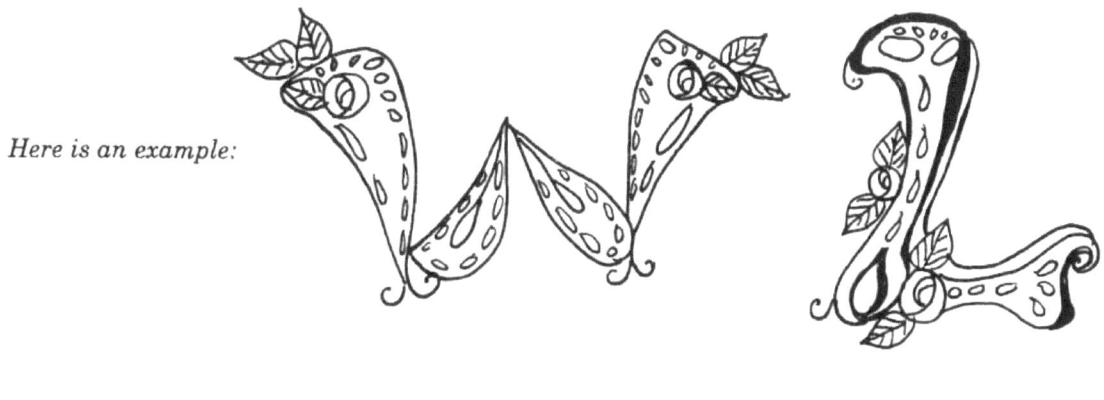

Would you make one like mine as well as one of your own?

Part 6 PASLEY

PLP

The Pasley consists of the same type of holes in the Eyelet and the Windows. The Pasley is a pattern of "holes" which are colored in not left blank. Close attention to the coloring can make beautiful designwork in your lettering. There again "the Pasley print" in fabrics can give you inspiration in designing your letters.

Here are just a few examples:

Could you please try a few?

Part 7 ROPES and TRIMS

Ropes are a cute add-on to a letter or letter picture. Whether you are lining a letter on the inside or outside with a rope or extending a bit of rope out into the picture around the letters the rope starts with a single line. Within and around the letters the line is drawn after the basic letter is drawn. The rope is an add-on. Within this single line drawn right next to the letter evenly you may draw a pattern of rope lines with a fine tipped black ink gel pen. Another way to draw rope is to extend it out into the surroundings of your letters. This is done by adding a second line parallel to the first line. Keep it as even as possible. When the 2 lines are dry fill the double line in with a rope pattern of lines.(shown below) The first line that is drawn needs some forthought before you draw it. Think to yourself," where would this rope help this picture?"

The easiest rope seems to be straight lines at an angle drawn like this:

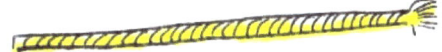

PLP

Could you try drawing rope like this?

This is a sample of ropes drawn with a curve:

Would you try a rope with some curve to it?

Here is a letter "lined with rope" (very useful in "Cowboy Expressions")

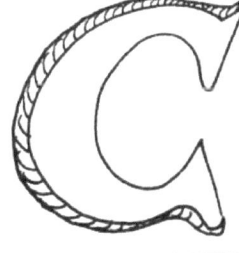

Would you try lining this letter with a rope?

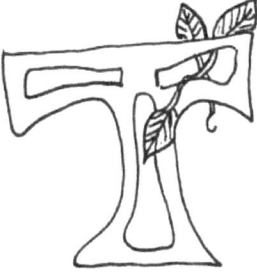

Rope can either have that "single strand look" or a more complicated pattern like this one.

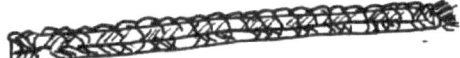

PLP

You may develope one you like better. Experiment!
Remember to let your ink gel ink dry a few minutes before coloring the rope in.
I like to color it with a gold, yellow or gray colored pencil.
Try to make a bit of your favorite rope.

*TRIM can be drawn much like rope around your letters with other patterns.
Be willing to try such inventive trims. These trims need to be an add-on done after the main letter formation.
Here are a few to consider:

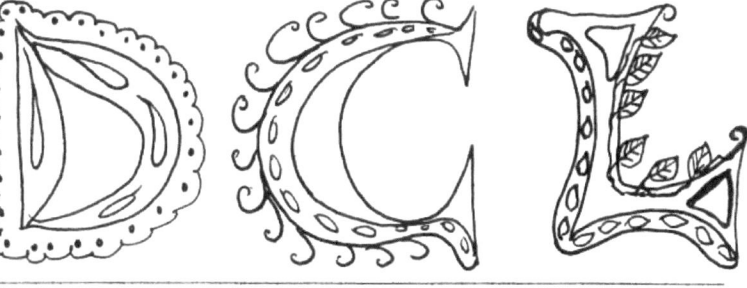

Care to try some trim on this letter?

Would you like to try some of your own?

PLP

**** AN IMPORTANT EMBELLISHMENT TIP
   The Metalic and Glitter ink gel pens are very beautiful to use on top of or lining other coloring. Give it a try on your practice paper.

Lesson 7 SHADOWING AND DIMENSIONING

In order to add the illusion of depth to your letters a line on one side or the other will add this touch. (Keep to one side in your entire drawing. You are showing where the light source in nature is coming from) You need to fill in this space inside the dimension line with either a solid dark coloring, a slightly shaded coloring or a pattern that brings the letter a look of depth. The solid shading of this area with a regular black felt pen is one technique I use. Slanted lines in a pattern, dots in a pattern, a light shadow of gray or a highlighting yellow color will work well also to make this illusion of depth.

Here are just a few examples:

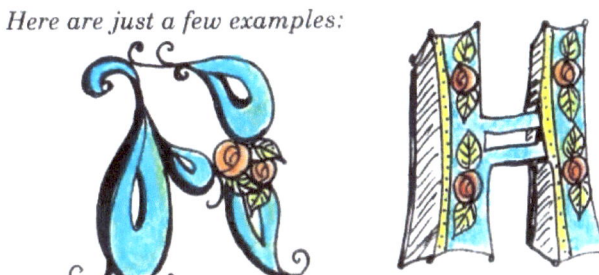

Could you try one of each of these examples,

Lesson 8 DESIGNER LETTERING

Designer Lettering is done by first drawing the form of a letter. Then go back and add curly lines, embellishments, dimensional lines and nature drawings. This is also the way cursive living letters are done. Depending on the theme of your word the features can vary with great imaginative drawing additions.

Here are just a few examples.

A designer loop is made by forming your basic letter first and then going back and adding on to it.
Here is an example of this style:
This S is made with a simple stroke of the pen to begin with.

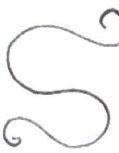

Try one of your own:

Then I go back and add what I call "designing art" or "designing touches".
It begins to take on slowly more and more character.

Try one like this one:

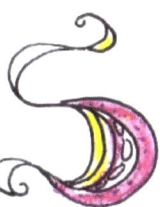

After I achieve a simple look, I decide whether I want to add Depth Lines(3-D). They will be on one side of the letter.

Create your letter S and add Depth lines on one side only. (It will be up to you which side you want the light to be from)

Now first draw an S with the Depth line on the left and then one with the Depth line on the right.

Try going back and coloring them in similarly to the one colored here. You choose the colors.

PLP

Let's try the letter P

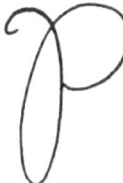

Try it 3 times.

Now try adding Designer Loops.

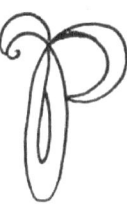

Now add Depth Lines.

Add your embellishments from Nature and Designer Touches...

Try some dashes(like stitches), 2 roses(anywhere you like on the letter). some eyelet and some curlys.

PLP

CURSIVE INSTRUCTION

I would like to now give instruction on Cursive Lettering in the "Living Letter" context.

Step 1
First write out the letter or words in a nice, careful cursive style.
Use your black ink gel pen. Let it dry.

Step 2
Go back on those letters and dress them up with designer loops and touches!
Depth lines, flowers, leavs and so forth...

Step 3
Color in the letters the way you like.

Here is an example of such a word brought through the letter development.

First:

Second:

Third:

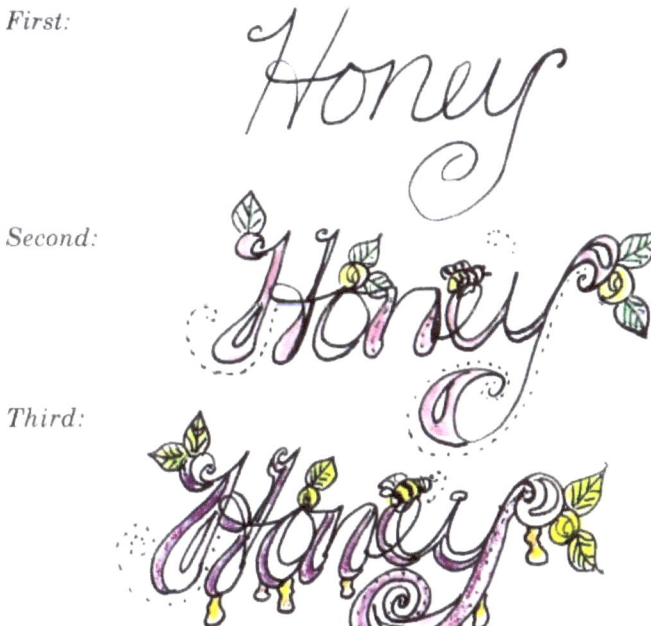

The embellishments or touches are up to you when you create your own letters. Pick and choose what you like.

Can you first draw a designer letter.

Can you now do a designer letter word with a theme?

Designer Letter "Animal Skins"

This is a very fun way to use lettering for young and old alike. Make your first letter in a big wide style with your black ink gel pen. You may either draw your other letters in that big style or make them a more plain printed style. Inside the big wide letter or letters color it with black felt pen and colored pencils to resemble an animal skin. First draw in the black areas and lines needed. Then use colored pencils(and or color crayons and felt pens) to create the areas around the black color.

Here are just a few examples:

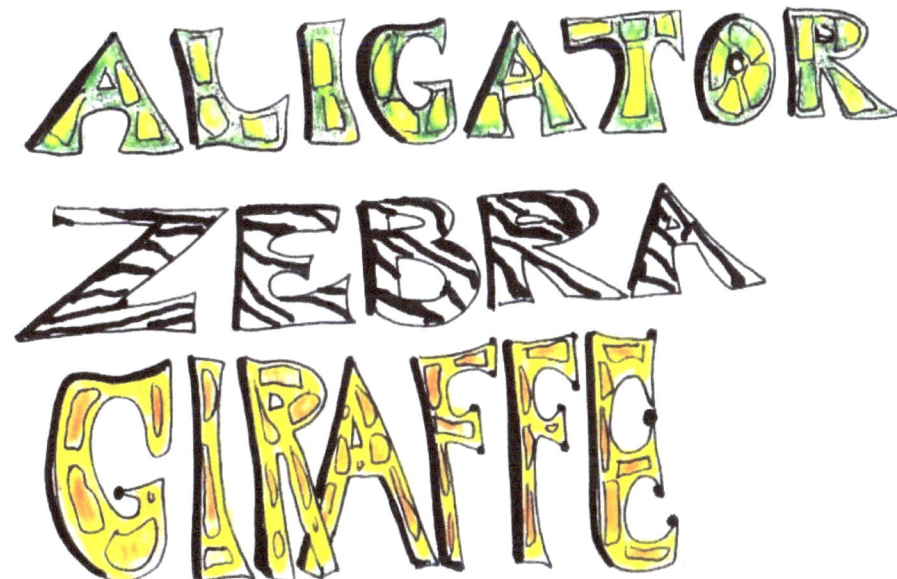

Would you try one of these?

Lesson 9 CREATIVE COLORING

This may become your favorite part of "Living Letters". The color choices are so important.
Before coloring the letters you are pleased with make a black and white copy(at least 1)
with a copier. You may want to save back your "original" and begin coloring your copy. This way you
will always have access to making another black and white copy to color in.
It is a way you can save up your originals and make "a coloring book" for others. Most of all it's a way
to experiment with different color combinations and coloring effects on your letters.

Now the funnest part of making "Living letters", THE COLORING!!!
Which colors should I use? On your copies of your original explore with different colors.
*Have colored pencils or crayons sharp enough to use and ready to go.
As you proceed to color"your" letters you will be making several other choices.

What fun it is to have "the say" on how something will look.
First of all always make sure your ink gel pen work is dry.(several seconds)
You will find some colors look very strong against other colors or even against blank spaces.You will
discover alot about negative and positive spaces. The negative spaces make the solid colored spaces"pop".
As you draw on in "Living Letter World" you will also appreciate the power of color and lines more
and more.

The RAINBOW EFFECT

This is something a friend of our family showed me. I named it the" Rainbow Effect". For a very special
effect on a word or several words try this technique.

Pick either the cool color spectrum or the warm color spectrum. Start at either the top or the bottom of
your already dry ink gel printed words. Color patches of the letter in the sequence of the warm or cool
colors order. For an example: start at the top of the letter with light yellow. Color a bit of this color, then
bright yellow, then yellow orangs, then orange, then red, then deep red. You can reverse the order or the
point you start from. You can do a cool color sequence just as well. It would be either from the blues to
the greens or the greens to the blues into the purples. Please see my examples and try several of your
own. It's one of my favorite things to do.(an eye pleaser)

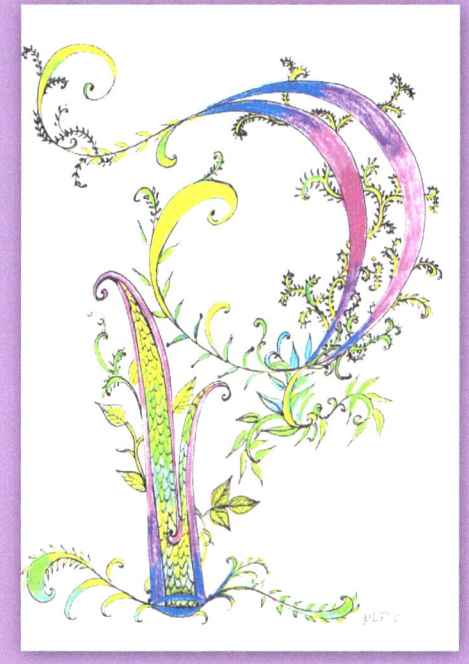
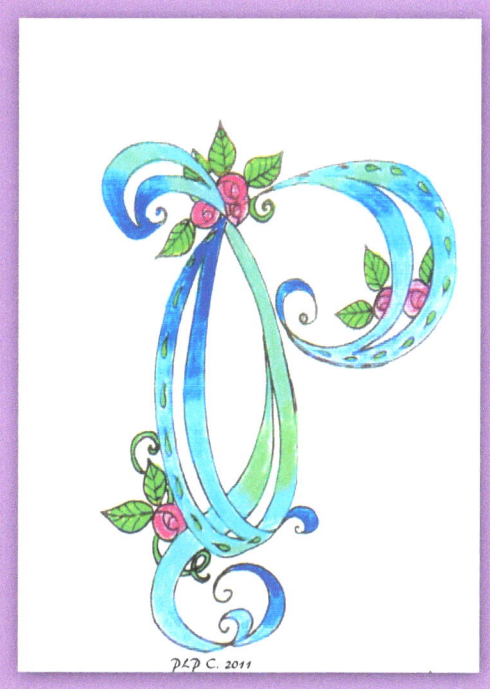
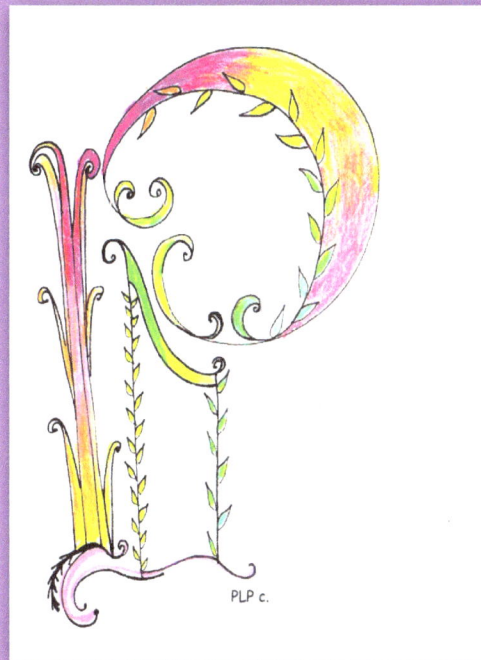
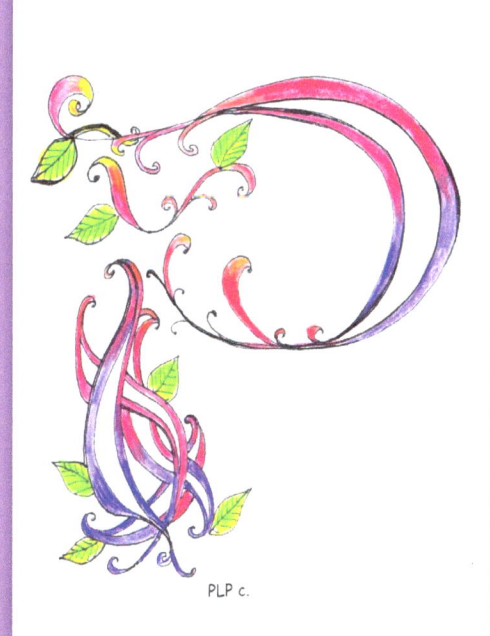

The Rainbow Effect

Lesson 11 NATURE TOUCHES

Whether you choose to draw simple or complex, abstract or realistic, it is the added features from nature that make our letters look alive. There's no end to what can be added in artform to enhance a letter, word or phrase. We will now look at just a few of the simple "Living Touches" that you can add to your lettering.

Part 1 Flowers

The simplest rose pattern shown earlier is a great addition to lettering. The rose could be drawn differently or the use of any other flower in nature can be put in it's place. A great way to get ideas for the simple forms of flowers is to look at the floral designs on material and embroidery work. For the best detailed flowers go right to the flower or a photograph of it in a gardening book and sketch it out on a separate paper. Be sure to always keep track of which leaf goes with which plant.

Here is "The Rose" and "The Violet"

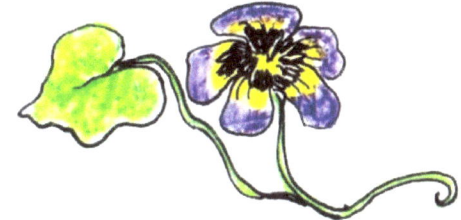

Could you try drawing each of these.

Part 2 Other Plants

Background grass, greenery, vines and trees can be very complimentary to lettering. My favorite thing to do is to draw the greenery either around a border surrounding the words and letters, or to wind it in and out thru the holes I have put in my letters. Ofcourse it can be quite an illusion of dimension and realism.

Here is an example of this:

PLP

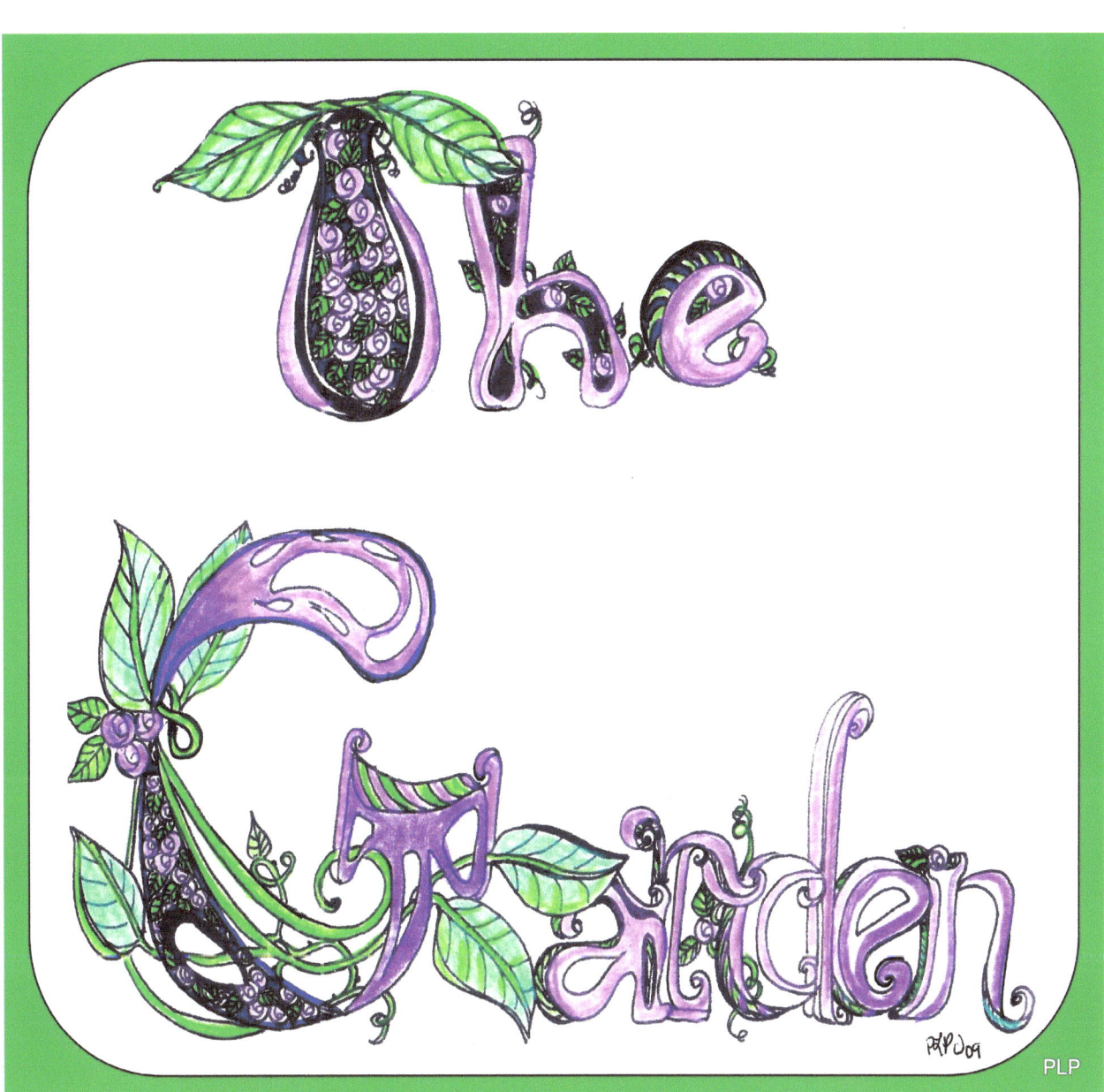

Give it a try.

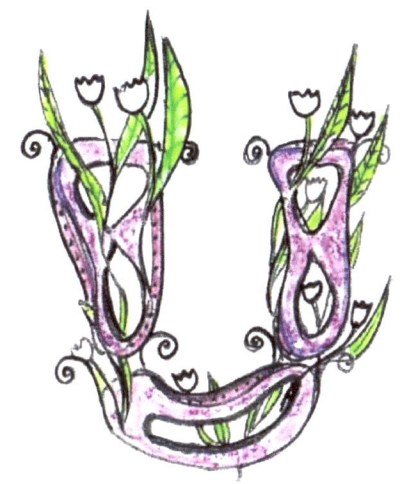

Part 3 Fruit

Fruit are fun to draw. They are an easy model to find in your home. They always bring alot of character and beauty to a lettering drawing. Again make sure to get the shape of the leaf correct for the kind of fruit you are drawing. Look up the fruit picture and practice sketching it without your letters first. Grape vines are especially fun to draw in and around things.

Here is an example:

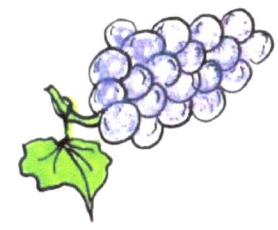

Would you try drawing a cluster of grapes?

Part 4 Insects

Insects are interesting to add on a lettering project. They can certainly add beauty and character to your lettering. Again looking up the shape and colors in a nature book is important if you want a realistic look. I like doing ants, ladybugs, butterflies and caterpillars. How about you?

Here is one example:

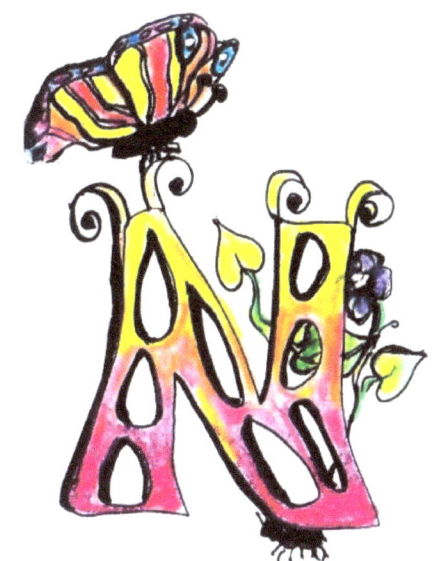

Try one of your own.

Part 5 Birds

Birds can sit on your letters adding special interest. They can fly around your letters.
Again sketch on a scratch paper first. Pay attention to detail whether you are being simplistic or realistic. Birds are a wonderful addition to lettering. They send a message of life and perhaps "song". Some birds (such as the dove) have a symbolic meaning to people.

Here is one example:

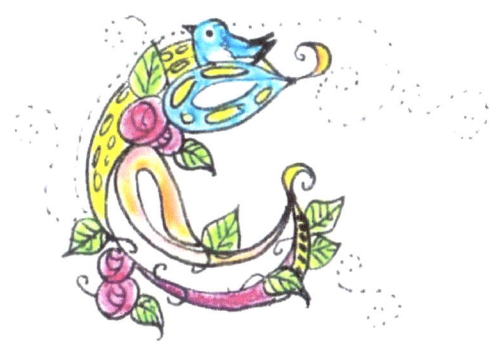

Would you like to try?

Living Letters

By Peggy Louise Parrish

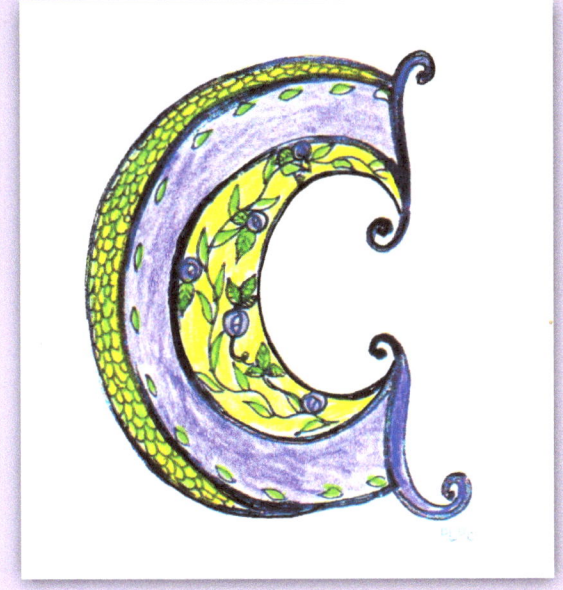
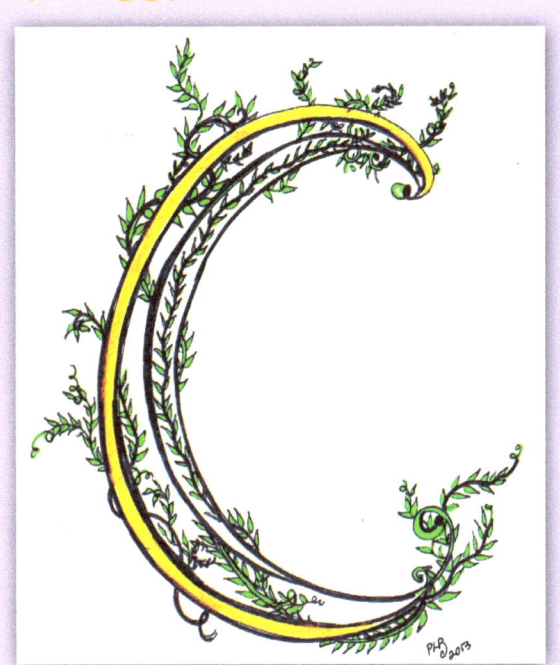
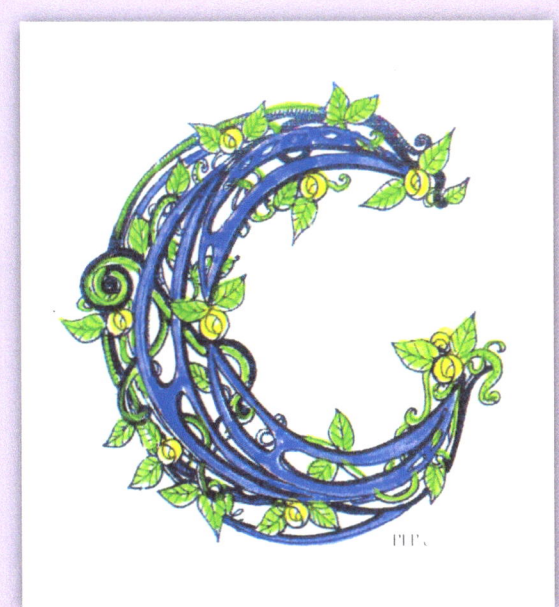
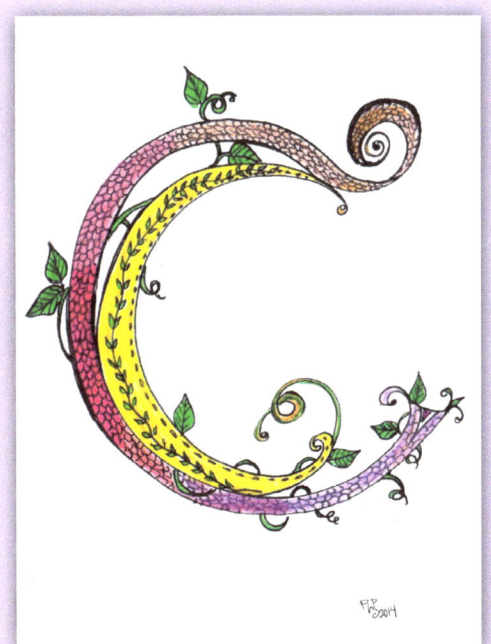

Endless Possibilities

PLP

*Doodle, doodle, doodle! Practice either your lettering techniques or your" Living Touches" whenever you have pockets of time. Keep a clipboard with blank paper and an ink gel pen nearby for those times you are restless, bored or waiting for someone. You can always color it in later when you are in a quiet coloring mood. Many wonderful ideas come when you are in your "inbetween times" and happen to be inspired by nature.

*LAST ASSIGNMENT
(optional)
If you have enjoyed the "Living Letters" experience try to make a whole alphabet to hold onto. Make copies of it while it is black and white. Color in one of the copies. Another option is to make each letter have one page and make it into a coloring alphabet book. Share it with others. Keep up your doodling and developing. There is no boundaries to what your very own alphabet style can become. Enjoy!

*Attention to details! If you are pleased with your letter sign your name with the date. If you are going to use it in public the word copyright with the date is important or the abreviation (c)20;8 with your name.

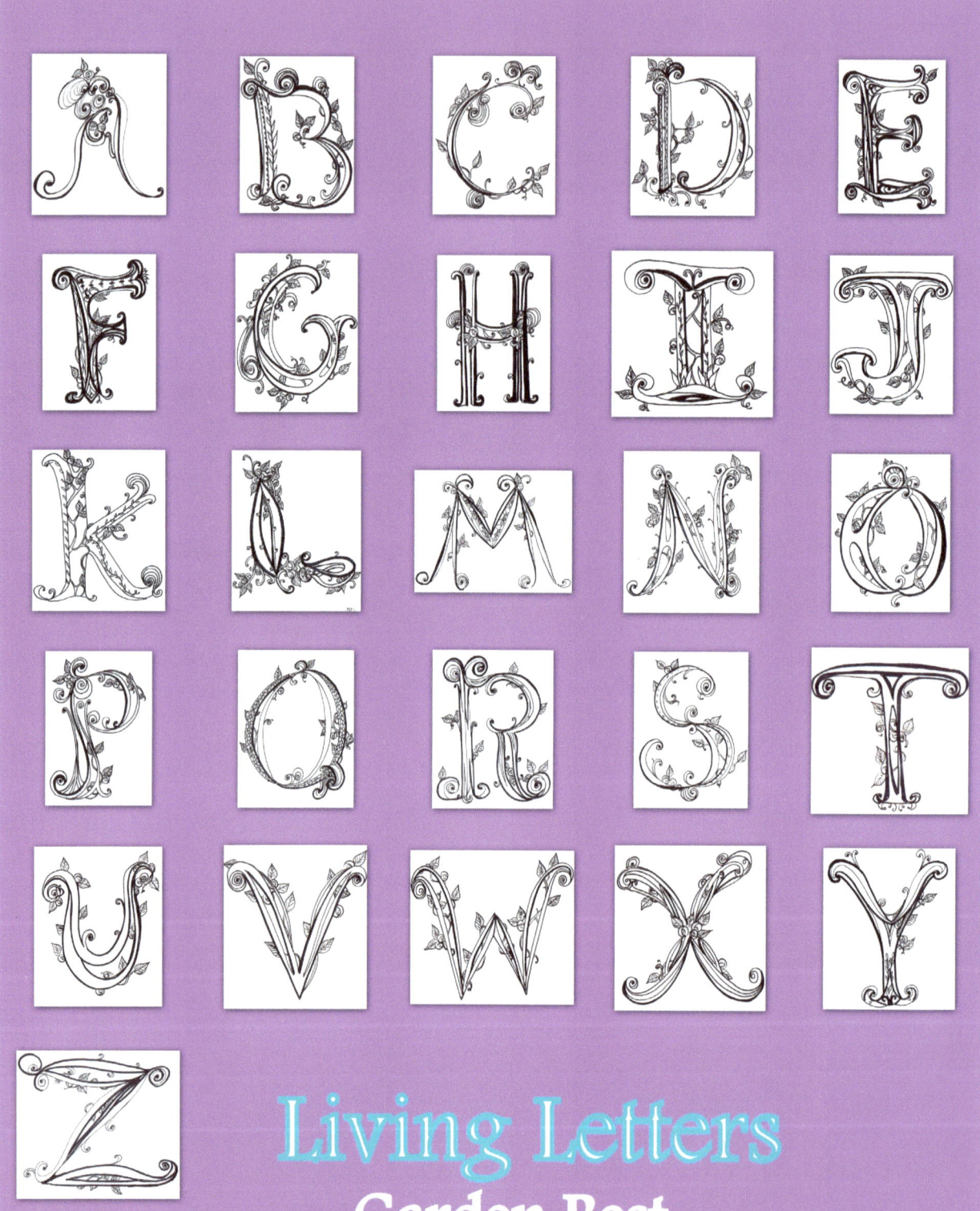

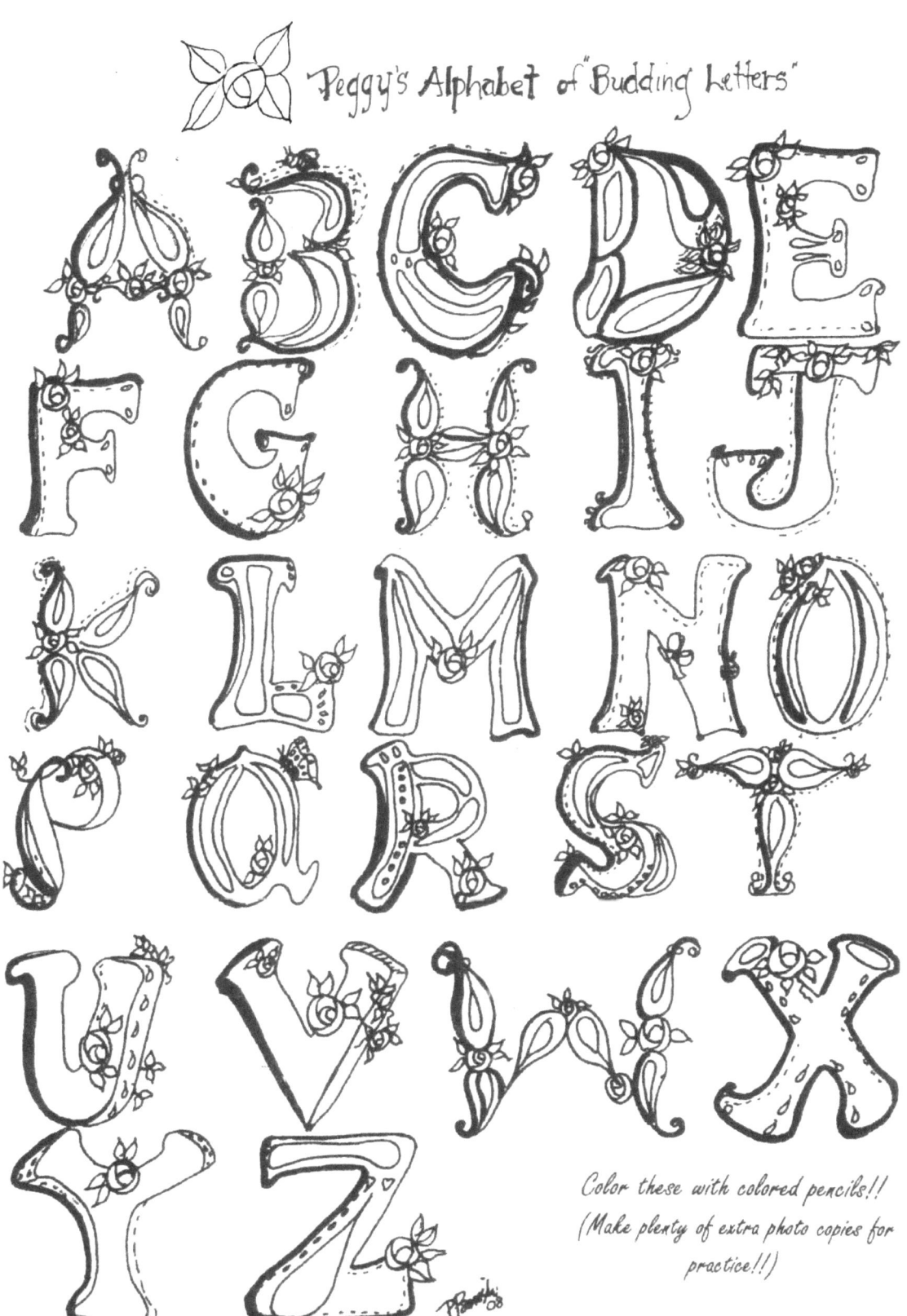

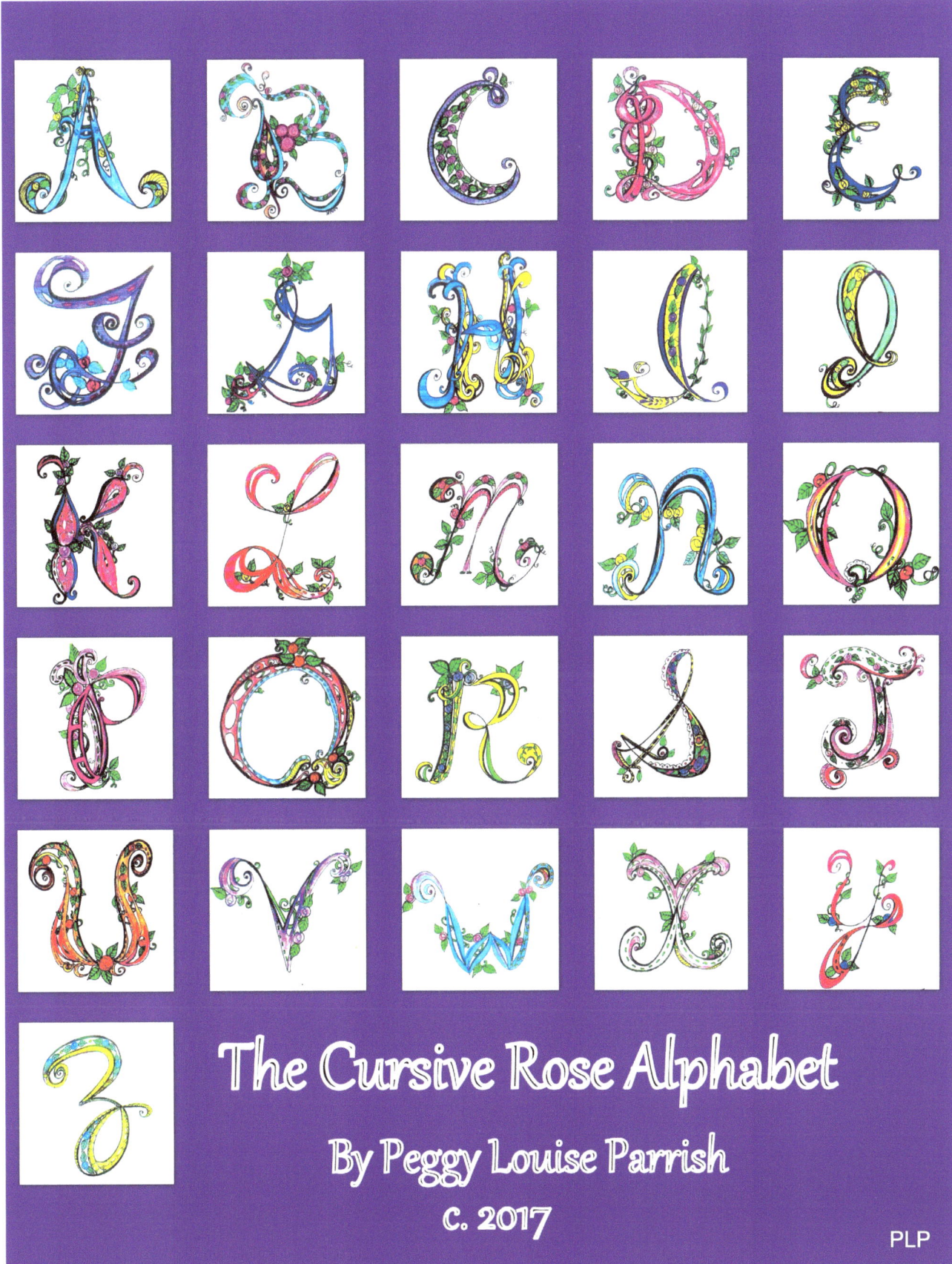

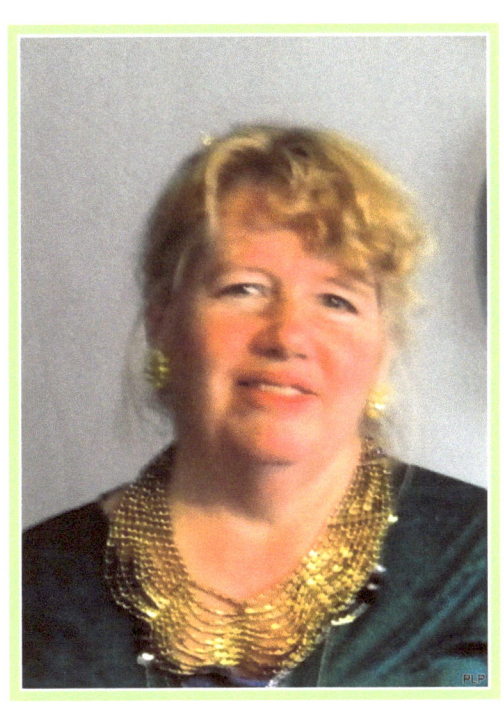

Artist Peggy Louise Parrish

This workbook called Living Letters Lesson was written and compiled in 2010. Since this time artist Peggy Louise Parrish has had a huge amount of creative fun developing letters. She has during 2017-2018 finished an unusual collection of over 500 original letters called Letter Wonders. Each letter in this series has it's own coloring book. The following page will show the names of these books. Most, (but not all) of these letters have some kind of "Living" plant or add-on inside or around them, qualifying them in her definition of "Living Letter" designs. Because these are a huge assortment of artsy letters, those of you who enjoy this workbook would probably enjoy checking out Peggy's series.

This book is a way to springboard into your very own style with add-ons. There is no end to where lettering can go. Let your own lettering develop from these lessons. Add your own favorite flowers, insects, vines and themes. Remember, "Practice makes Perfect". If you want to look up more of Peggy's artwork and writing look on Amazon.com under Peggy Louise Parrish books.

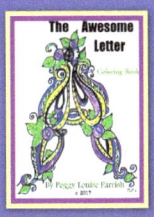 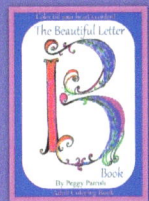 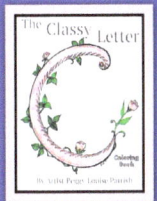 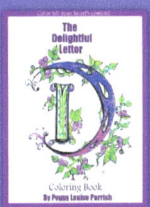 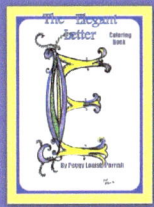
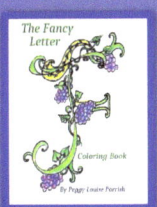 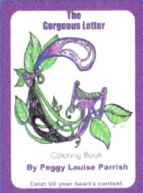 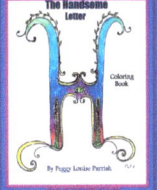 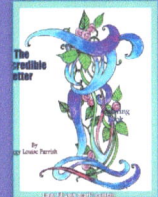 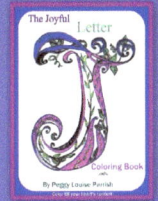
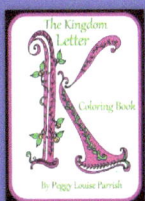 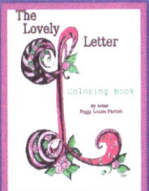 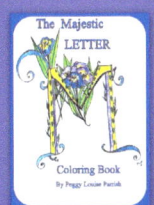 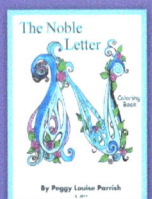 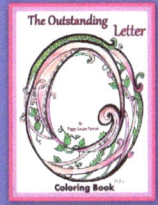
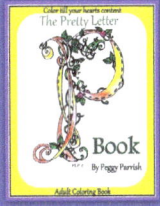 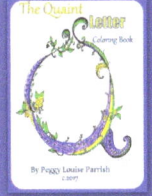 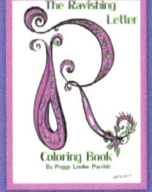 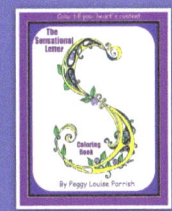 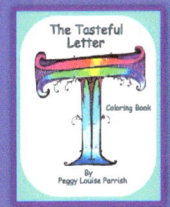
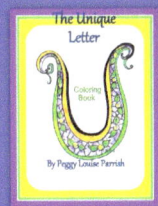 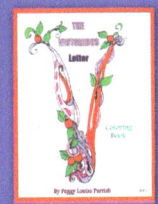 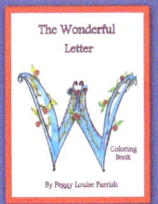 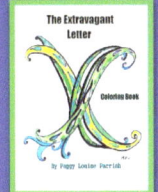 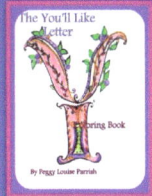
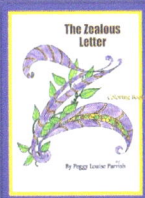

Letter Wonders
All letter Coloring Books
By Peggy Louise Parrish
C 2017

www.ingramcontent.com/pod-product-compliance
Lightning Source LLC
Chambersburg PA
CBHW051203220526
45473CB00003B/885